Dear Parent:
Your child's love of reading starts here!

Every child learns to read in a different way and at his or her own speed. Some go back and forth between reading levels and read favorite books again and again. Others read through each level in order. You can help your young reader improve and become more confident by encouraging his or her own interests and abilities. From books your child reads with you to the first books he or she reads alone, there are I Can Read Books for every stage of reading:

SHARED READING
Basic language, word repetition, and whimsical illustrations, ideal for sharing with your emergent reader

BEGINNING READING
Short sentences, familiar words, and simple concepts for children eager to read on their own

READING WITH HELP
Engaging stories, longer sentences, and language play for developing readers

READING ALONE
Complex plots, challenging vocabulary, and high-interest topics for the independent reader

ADVANCED READING
Short paragraphs, chapters, and exciting themes for the perfect bridge to chapter books

I Can Read Books have introduced children to the joy of reading since 1957. Featuring award-winning authors and illustrators and a fabulous cast of beloved characters, I Can Read Books set the standard for beginning readers.

A lifetime of discovery begins with the magical words **"I Can Read!"**

Visit www.icanread.com for information
on enriching your child's reading experience.

Paddington Plays On. Text copyright © 2016 by Michael Bond. Story adapted by Christy Webster from an original Paddington story written by Michael Bond. Illustrations copyright © 2016 by HarperCollins Publishers. All rights reserved. Manufactured in U.S.A. No part of this book may be used or reproduced in any manner whatsoever without written permission except in the case of brief quotations embodied in critical articles and reviews. For information address HarperCollins Children's Books, a division of HarperCollins Publishers, 195 Broadway, New York, NY 10007.
www.icanread.com

Library of Congress Control Number: 2015946549
ISBN 978-0-06-243071-7 (trade bdg.) — ISBN 978-0-06-243070-0 (pbk.)

Typography by Brenda E. Angelilli

20 21   CWM   10 9 8   ❖   First Edition

I Can Read!™ BEGINNING 1 READING

PADDINGTON
Plays On

Michael Bond
illustrated by R. W. Alley

HARPER

An Imprint of HarperCollinsPublishers

Paddington and the Browns
took a trip to France.
The people in the village
were excited to meet a young bear.
The baker made buns
just for Paddington.
Other shopkeepers waved to him
when he walked through town.

The next morning,
Paddington woke
to loud noises
in the street.

Paddington looked
out the window.
People were dressed
in fancy clothes.

The shops were decorated
with flags.
They were filled
with sweets and candles.

Paddington went to see the baker.

He told Paddington

all about a special festival

in the town.

That day, there would be a fair,
fireworks, and a parade!
"I am the leader of the band,
and this is my uniform,"
said the baker.
Paddington was very impressed.

Paddington and the Browns
went to the fair.
There was so much
to see and do!

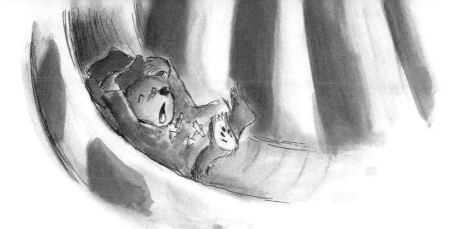

Paddington tried

the slides and swings.

He rode the merry-go-round

over and over again.

Next Paddington visited
a fortune-teller.
She looked into her crystal ball.
"You will go on a journey.
It will end with a bang!"
she predicted.

When Paddington came
out of the tent
he saw the baker
looking worried.

The band's drummer
was too sick to drum.
They needed a replacement!

"The fortune-teller predicted
a big bang," Paddington said.
"This could be it."
Paddington would join the band!

Boom, boom, boom!
Paddington practiced
with the band
all afternoon.

The parade began that evening.
The baker led the band
down the street.
Paddington came last.
He carried a big drum.
He could not see over it.

21

But everyone saw Paddington!
The people were thrilled that he
was playing in the band.
He had saved the day!

Everyone clapped.

The Browns clapped the loudest.

Paddington beamed with pride.

The band turned
at the end of the street.

But Paddington kept marching.

He did not see the band turn.

He just kept playing his drum.

Paddington was tired.

His hat kept slipping

into his eyes.

He could not hear the band anymore.

The drum was getting heavy.

Paddington tripped and fell down.

He could not get up!

Thump, thump, thump.

Paddington kept drumming.

The Browns watched
the band pass by.
Where was Paddington?
They followed the sound of his drum.
They were so glad to find him!

Everyone was thrilled
to see Paddington.
They cheered for
their guest drummer.

Paddington and the Browns
settled in to watch
the evening show.
Fireworks!

Bang! The sky filled with colors.

Paddington beamed.

It was the perfect ending

to an eventful day.